THE PADGATE STORY:
1946 – 2006

Written and compiled

by

Elsie Newton

on behalf of
Padgate Old Students' Association

University of Chester

First published 2007
by Corporate Communications
University of Chester
Parkgate Road
Chester CH1 4BJ

Printed and bound in the UK by the
Print Unit
University of Chester
Designed by the
Graphics Team
University of Chester

ISBN   978-1-905929-31-3

Dedication

This book is dedicated to everyone who has been a part of the Padgate family since 1946, and who shared the many experiences with us.

Particularly, we dedicate it to Betty Moisley. She was a member of the Experienced Teachers' Course, which opened the permanent College in 1949. She was the driving force behind the founding of Padgate Old Students' Association, at Miss Martin's instigation. Betty's notes about the early days were the motivation for the research that eventually led to the production of this book. She was a Vice-President of POSA and an active member of the Executive Committee up to the time of her death in January 2007. She will be sadly missed by the many who knew her.

Foreword

By the Vice-Chancellor of the University of Chester

Chester and Warrington have enjoyed a close and productive relationship in the provision of higher education in the North-West of England ever since "the Great Diocesan Meeting", which led to the foundation of Chester College, was held in the National School House in Warrington on the 25th January 1839. When Padgate College was founded, shortly after World War II, it rapidly developed into an institution with marked similarities to Chester, and the two colleges evolved along parallel paths during the 1950s and 1960s.

Following the major re-organisation of teacher education in the 1970s, those paths diverged somewhat; but when times changed and a larger institution was needed in the region, it seemed natural that Chester and Padgate should join together, forming a united College of Higher Education that soon became the University of Chester.

The history of higher education in Chester has already been ably documented in the publications of the former Deputy Principal John L. Bradbury, our Dean of Academic Quality and Standards Professor Graeme J. White and Ian Dunn, the County Librarian of Cheshire. It is therefore enormously pleasing that Elsie Newton and other members of the POSA Committee have been willing to produce the current history of Padgate and so commemorate this other strand of our joint heritage.

However, this is not just a history of Padgate College. It also tells the story of the development of the Padgate Old Students' Association; and what shines through the text is the affection with which former Padgate students hold their *alma mater*, together with their gratitude for the educational experiences it gave them. Such affection provides a fitting tribute to Padgate's strengths as an institute of higher education; one on which I am sure staff at our Warrington campus will be able to build in future years.

Canon Professor T. J. Wheeler DL

CONTENTS

IN THE BEGINNING...

A former camp for Canadian servicemen, at Fearnhead, about three miles north-east of Warrington, was selected by Lancashire County Education Committee as a suitable site for an emergency training college. The site covered approximately 40 acres, contained a variety of buildings and was situated on the main bus route from Warrington to Leigh. Padgate Railway Station was situated about midway between the site and the RAF camp at Padgate. It was intended as a college for about 360 male students, demobbed from the armed services and intending to enter the teaching profession. Known locally then – and for many years afterwards – as 'Canada Hall', the College opened its doors in 1946. The Principal was G. Harrison, MA. The H-shaped blocks became mainly residential accommodation and the collection of other buildings was transformed into administration, teaching and catering areas. Rumour had it that at least one world-famous American star had entertained the Canadians in the very fine theatre on the site! The last group of ex-service men moved out at Easter 1949. They held one Reunion at Whitsuntide the same year.

PADGATE...

In 1949 the Ministry of Education recognised the College as permanent, providing two year teacher training courses exclusively for women and the College was a constituent member of the School of Education in the University of Manchester. Joyce Martin, BA, was appointed founder Principal of Padgate Training College, with a remit to establish precisely this. So, on the 1st June 1949, a group of 98 "Experienced Teachers", women who despite their teaching experience were now required to gain a qualification to teach, walked through the gates for the first time. They were about to embark upon a special short, but intensive, course of study, aimed at enabling them to achieve qualified teacher status, and to continue within the profession.

It was a motley group of uncertificated serving teachers that formed the Experienced Teachers' Course. Among them were three grandmothers, some war widows, previously failed two year students and several single women.

It was decided that the College colours would be red and white on black. The shield-shaped badge featured a central flaming torch, with a heraldic beast to either side. The red rose of Lancashire was placed either side of the flame. Below the shield, a streamer bore the words of the College motto – *Sagax Semper Discit* - generally translated by the non-Latin experts among us as, "The wise are always learning".

The student residential blocks were lettered from A to K. The H-shaped single-storey buildings housed bath and shower rooms, a boiler room and an entrance in the cross-section. Single student rooms occupied the four wings and the tutors were housed in small flatlets at the end of each wing. Some of the married tutors and their families also lived in the flats, while others were housed in a separate building. Each room contained a bed, table, chair, single wardrobe and a small cupboard. Books could be kept on a shelf above the table. There was a wash-basin below the small window. Each door had a Yale lock, and there was a charge for the loan of a master key from the Matron if a student lost her key or locked herself out. Devious means were employed

A social gathering of staff and former staff members from the 1950s, including former Principals George Harrison and Joyce Martin.

to open the door without traipsing across to the Sick Bay, and the more agile used the window to gain access, particularly if arriving back after "Check-in Time". There was a warm community feeling among residents of the blocks and groups of friends would often gather in someone's room for supper. At one period, competitions were held to find the best-kept block garden. As summer approached, students returned from home visits bearing boxes of plants and cuttings, garnered from their families' gardens. If the comical site of students crawling over the grass wielding scissors could be seen, then Judgement Day was nigh!

At this time, each newly arriving student was paired up with a member of the previous Course – her "College Mother". It was the College Mother's job to help her "Daughter" to feel welcome, to settle in and to find her way around the strange new world of College. She was usually in the same Personal Group as her "Daughter". Every student belonged to a Personal Group, and regular meetings were held with the Personal Tutor. These were often held in the Tutor's flat, and some tutors organised a supper for their group once a term, so students, tutors and family members got to know one another. Students paid the princely sum of 2s. 6p, equivalent to 12 $^1/_2$ pence today, as subscription to the Students' Council, which had an Executive comprised of members elected by the students who were resident in each block.

All students were expected to be back in College by "Check-in Time". These times were 10 pm (Sunday to Thursday), 10.20 pm (Friday), and 10.40 pm (Saturday) and coincided with the arrival of the bus from Warrington. A student from each block was "Duty Student" for the day. She had to report to the Duty Tutor in the Administration building that all the students in her block were present in their rooms. This was not the most popular job, as it entailed trailing across the site at the respective times, and it seemed to be wet, cold or blowing a gale for most of the year. The site was open, and, at the time, Crab Lane was a country lane with a ditch alongside, and open fields beyond. At the beginning of each year, the Second Year students put on a concert for the newcomers, to welcome them to College. In 1956, "I Love Paris" was a popular song of the day. So a parody was written for the concert, the words of which began:

I love Padgate in the summer, when it drizzles,
I love Padgate in the fall, when it's raining,
I love Padgate,
Why oh why do I love Padgate?
Because it's raining here!

Lectures took place each morning and from 4 pm to 6 pm. It was then a scramble to get ready for the formal evening meal, with the "Duty Student" for the day sitting at the Top Table. The afternoon was the time for various games and other activities. Students were also expected to join at least two of the various societies that existed. Drama, Choir and Country Dancing were three popular ones. The Drama Society rehearsed and presented a variety of plays in the theatre. Dorothy Peach, a tutor of English, was the Producer/Director, and she always seemed to get the best out of her actors. The costumes were a work of art in themselves. From a distance, they appeared to be made from the finest of fabrics and embroideries, but in reality they were made from dozens of yards of calico and other basic materials. This was all down to the skill of Kay Herring, the Craft Tutor, who was a fine painter in her own right, and whose paintings were displayed and sold in galleries in London. She designed both costumes and scenery, and led her team of non-acting society members to produce first class results every time. The productions were always outstanding.

The College Choir, under the able direction of Joan Alban, entered the Youth Choirs section of the Llangollen International Musical Eisteddfod each year. That was a thrilling experience for the Choir members, who were also able to appreciate hearing choirs and soloists of all ages from many different parts of the world once they had finished singing.

During the first term and a half, students were also expected to attend lectures on Saturday mornings. Blocks of approximately six weeks were allocated to the "basic" subjects of mathematics, librarianship, nature study, and so on. All were considered essential for the classroom teacher. During the days leading up to periods of school practice, the library was a hive of industry during afternoons and evenings, as students queued to produce visual aids using the methods then available – projector and gel. Pictures were projected on to a large sheet of paper and card, the outlines drawn in and then taken away and coloured in and labelled. Writing on to a bed of a special

The full cast from the production of *The Hopeful Travellers* in February 1956.

gel reproduced written work. How pleased everyone was when Roneo duplicating machines became available.

In the early 1950s, some foodstuffs were still rationed or in short supply. So, on the morning of the first day of observation or teaching practice, students each collected a packet of tea and sugar to donate to the staff room supplies of the school they were attending.

Dances were held regularly at the College. In order to compensate for the lack of male students, men were invited from the Padgate RAF camp and the Atomic Energy establishment at Risley, as were police cadets from Bruche and boy-friends of students. There were usually one or two American servicemen who were also stationed in the area. At least one student is reputed to have become a "GI Bride", as British women who married American servicemen were known as at this time. Men, whether they were family members or friends, could not be entertained in students' rooms without written permission from parents.

During the early 1950s, the College magazine *Sagax* was introduced, and issued annually. It was the successor to *Padgate Post*, the wall newspaper that had appeared periodically during the first year of Padgate. *Sagax*, with a cover design featuring a wise old owl, contained a foreword written by the Principal, reports on the activities of the various societies and news of the progress of several College teams. Poems and short essays written by the students were also included.

Eileen Coulson (née Callear) has fond memories of her time as a student between 1952 and 1954:

I greatly enjoyed my time at Padgate. I loved having my own room, and was sorry to leave it behind. Particular memories include having to ask my parents to write to

College giving permission for me to entertain my boy-friend (now my husband of 50 years) in my room! Three meals a day were provided in the Dining Room, but if we were hungry and needed to fill up there was always a huge pot of strawberry jam and sliced bread and butter in each "block". We had to be in by 10 pm each night and were only allowed one weekend away (to go home) during each half-term. My mother and father would send me a ten-shilling note every week for pocket money, which was spent on stamps, bus fares, etc.

I was in the College Choir, which entered the Llangollen International Musical Eisteddfod competition, although we did not win! There was also a coach from College on the Wednesday of the Eisteddfod week for the folk dancing. To see that and the various costumes and to be able to talk to so many people from so many different lands was a memorable experience – foreign travel then was not common. (My first trip abroad was after I was married!)

I remember, too, Miss Alban with whom I studied Music, and Miss Wright, whose bedroom was next to mine at the end of the block. My coughing disturbed her so much one night that she complained and had me sent to the Sick Bay, where I remained for some days.

During 1955-57, work began on the building of the first of the new, purpose designed, multi-storey Halls of Residence, each one housing about 50 students. Members of the 1955-57 Course were the first to move in from the H Block, to be joined by members of the 1956-58 Course. There was also a close for tutors' houses near to the Main Entrance on Fearnhead Lane and to the College Chapel. This was used for Sunday services and also for other services during the week.

Janet Hobbs (née Appleyard) was a student at that time, 1956-58, and intended to make her mark:

I tried to start a new tradition of singing carols on the last evening of term in December 1957. Christmas 1957 was the first year that the "New Blocks", as we called them, on both sides of the central area, were occupied, though at that time it was still a building site.

Lists of carols were given out and at 9pm groups gathered on the balconies to sing their way through the list, each hall trying to sing the loudest. We began together, but did not always end together, giving a pleasant echoing effect. Now, I understand the balconies cannot be used – maybe we put them under too much strain in 1957. Happy days – mostly.

Janet also had special dietary requirements, and found that College was not really at the forefront of the movement where menus were concerned:

During 1956-58, I was one of only two vegetarians in College. Every lunch-time we

Principal Joyce Martin and staff members Mr Birch, Mr White, Mr Howarth, Mr Thomas, Mr Aitcheson and Mr Barlow, as well as representatives from Seddon (the Builders), at the site of the new staff housing, 1955-57.

were served a cold plate of lettuce, one tomato and a pile of grated cheese. That was all. For our evening meal we received exactly the same - every day, twice a day, for two years. The only variation came when it was my turn to dine at the Head Table with Miss Martin and the staff. Amazingly, my salad was augmented with grated carrot and four apricot halves (tinned). This took some preparation and most of the staff had finished their food before mine arrived. I had to eat mine carefully as Miss Martin and others asked questions about my diet. Not an enjoyable experience.

When I entered College I weighed eight stones, but the "vegetarian" diet caused my weight to drop to seven stones – and I am 5' 7" tall. College did try to make amends by arranging for a daily pint of milk for me. My friends were happy to share it with me in their teas and coffees at supper-time.

The other "veggie" was in the year ahead of me. She was a member of the Salvation Army, I think, but I cannot recall her name. I wonder if she remained vegetarian. I did, and am still one today.

Janet Appleyard wrote a poem at the time describing her progression through the educational system. The poem was published originally in the College magazine, *Sagax*:

ADVICE

They told me that school was the place to have fun,
Where the days seemed to fly by – not go one by one,
But I found only plenty of work to be done.
All night,
All day,
All work,
No play.

They told me the sixth form would bring grace and poise,
Would teach me some manners and to refrain from noise,
But alas, I was guilty of ragging the boys.
Me! Poise
Or grace!
Not with
My face!

They told me that teaching was the noblest art,
Their glowing accounts made me so keen to start,
But it was just an excuse to make me depart.
Two years
Away!
Good show!
They say.

They told me that Padgate's a wonderful place
Filling all the young ladies with knowledge and grace,
But the waste of our talents is just a disgrace.
You can have
No fun,
While there's work
To be done.

Vera Singleton (née Woods), Mavis Fielding (née Tranter) and Norma Cousins (née Crockett), members of the 1956-58 Course, racked their brains for memories and incidents. Among the list of items the women took to College were a serviette and ring, which were stored in pigeonholes in the Dining Room and used each mealtime. Getting up at 6 am in order to catch a coach leaving at 6.45 am for schools in the Bolton/Chorley area for Teaching Practice was no fun, particularly as it meant arriving back equally late, with notes and planning to do for the next day. Did they still take a packet of tea and sugar for the staffroom on the first day, as was the custom earlier in the 1950s?

They moved into the "New Blocks" (i.e. halls of residence) during their second year at College. They were astounded by the luxury of the accommodation after the

Students, some wearing the Padgate College scarf, wait to board the coach that will take them to teaching practice in Horwich, Bolton.

tiny rooms in the old ex-service blocks. The Heals' curtains, furnishings and individual wash-basins were declared to be "fabulous". They celebrated 21st birthdays with daring bottles of cider and a buffet prepared in the new hall of residence kitchens.

Bouffant skirts were all the rage, with net petticoats underneath stiffened with sugar and water. Meanwhile, every student had to have a dress for dance, with matching knickers, all in radiant colours, and PE shorts that had to reach down to the knee.

Reference has already been made to rules concerning the entertaining of boy-friends, or any other male for that matter, in students' rooms. Vera remembers with great clarity the events of one visit by her boy-friend! She was busily running her bath in preparation for meeting him later in the day. He arrived early and Vera's friends went to tell her. She panicked – he was too early! THE RULES! She went to get him out of her room, forgetting there was no overflow in the bath, and was followed down the corridor by her overflowing bath water. Fortunately, her friends helped her mop up, and as far as we know, the rest of the visit passed off happily.

Pat Eagles, of the same Course, clearly remembers getting up early to travel to Llangollen to sing in the Ladies' Choir and the Youth Choir competitions. Although unsuccessful, she and her fellow Choir members enjoyed the international atmosphere. Miss Alban, Mr Pryce-Jones and the accompanists had worked hard to raise the choir to the highest possible standard. Pat herself was Choir rehearsal pianist from 1957 to 1958. Her lasting memory is of the banks of flowers in the huge marquee. She also remembers the choir attending the Remembrance Day Service at RAF Padgate.

The first small cohort of male students entered College in 1957. Things had to change and rules were relaxed, for obvious reasons. At least two of the males married fellow-students and they remain together today. The number of male students increased in the following years and the intake has remained mixed ever since. The student body as a whole remained fairly small, and did not rise above 250 until 1960.

Dave Stacey and Andy Slater were male students at Padgate during the 1960s and recall some comical times. Pranks were often played on the campus aimed at students, teachers and even librarians. Dave Stacey remembers how one prank involved soaking a student's room with water. Luckily, when the student returned he had been drinking for several hours, failed to notice the water and went straight to sleep!

An aerial view of the Padgate site taken in 1960 shows seven halls of residence situated in two rows leading down towards the Main Entrance on Fearnhead Lane, with a large grassed area between. The short row of tutors' houses can also be seen, plus a considerable number of the original H Blocks, which were still in existence. Apart from housing along both sides of the main road, the College was still in a rural area. Behind College, Crab Lane was essentially a country lane, with a ditch that ran alongside the fields. This was popular with students, particularly during the Nature Study course, when pond dipping expeditions and plant identification exercises were held.

The first College Rag Day was held in Warrington in 1960. £1,000 was raised, which was a great achievement for a small college.

By now, the two year course leading to the Teacher's Certificate had been extended to three years. All students studied the theory and practice of Education and two main academic subjects, chosen from a list of 16. These were: English Literature; History; Geography; French; German; Divinity; Social Studies; Mathematics; Physics; Chemistry; Rural Science; Biology; Drama; Art; Music; and Physical Education. Students also followed courses in curriculum and teaching methods to prepare them for work in the classroom. The College had self-contained and well-equipped facilities

An aerial view of Padgate Training College, 1960.

for Art, Music, Drama and PE. The Drama Studio had a working theatre and ancillary rooms. The large Gymnasium could be divided into two areas by screens for two different activities to take place at the same time.

Cyril Bailey, known to everyone in those days as "Sid" and now answering to the name of "Bill", was at Padgate from 1961 to 1964. He has fond memories of the place, as this essay shows:

As the Leigh Corporation bus approached Fearnhead, one conductor used to shout, "Padgate Holiday Camp!" I do not know where he got his inside information from, but he was right; for me, Padgate was three years holiday at the public's expense. I had been to a boys' grammar school and then spent a year at university reading Chemistry – or rather, not reading it, which is why I failed all my examinations and ended up at Padgate.

I came from a working-class background – a two-up, two-down terraced house, with one cold tap and no bathroom, where I had to share a bedroom with two brothers. This meant that Padgate and Heaven were indistinguishable. I had my own room with central heating, a hand-basin with hot and cold running water, new furniture, a comfortable bed with bedside lamp and, in my third year, a balcony and window box. Immediately outside my room was a bathroom. Downstairs was a lounge with settees, coffee tables and a piano. The food was free, and in the hostel kitchen there was fresh milk, cocoa, bread, butter and strawberry jam. My Local Education Authority also gave me a grant of £29 a term, which was more than enough for my cigarettes and beer.

There were girls galore, all of whom were interesting and some of whom were absolutely gorgeous. It was the period immediately after the publication of "Lady Chatterley's Lover", which symbolised the beginning of the end of the 1950s way of life. Everything was up to be challenged.

Formal ballroom dancing was on its way out and rock and roll was the order of the day. There were proper dances on some Saturday nights, but we had our own records and record player, and jived away Friday evenings in the Small Lounge. I never mastered ballroom dancing, but I got the hang of rock and roll – at least if I had a partner who knew the moves. Then one summer a group called The Beatles took the world by storm and all my moves were negated overnight. You just stood there, and shook yourself in whatever way took your fancy; you no longer held the girl in your arms or swung her at the end of arm's reach.

Having been for a year at university, where you came and went as you liked, I could not believe that Padgate took its "in loco parentis" role seriously. The first morning I went to the Hall for assembly. The Principal, Miss Martin, entered, in gown and mortarboard, walked to the stage and said: "Good morning, College". When the assembled students replied: "Good morning Miss Martin," in ragged unison, I had the feeling that I had somehow gone back to being a school-child – in a girls' school.

After "the announcements", Don Burrows the music tutor played "The Interlude" and the Catholic students left. Bereft of this group we were now free to sing hymns and pray. That was my first – and last – assembly.

As the term wore on the crowds thinned, so the Authorities decided to have a check-up. The Principal announced that all students were to go to their tutor groups immediately after assembly, where their personal tutors would make a note of who was there. One of the students could run really fast and was round the hostel waking us all up within seconds of the announcement. Within minutes of it, we were all in our tutor groups having our names recorded. How they managed to reconcile the full attendance record with the depleted assembly I do not know. But they must have realised that Authority's days were numbered. We were the third year of male intake and now that each year was fully mixed the nonsense had to go.

There was a night-time ritual called "Checking-in". We had to be in our rooms at 10.30 pm, standing to attention by our single occupancy beds, to have our names and presence recorded by the student who was lumbered with this duty for the week. The student then took the list to the night porter, and was expected to tell him who was missing. Since closing time at the "Farmers Arms" was also 10.30 pm, with ten minutes drinking-up time and a few minutes walk back to College, no one, except the sick and the duty student was in at "Checking-in Time". The duty student then had a dilemma. If he told the night porter who was out, he risked being beaten up by the drinkers for getting them into trouble; if he reported them in and someone was dead in a ditch, he would also be in trouble. The cost-benefit analysis meant that the night porter was always told that everyone was in at 10.30 pm. Then he watched as, over the next hour, droves of us drifted back from the pub.

You could take girls back to your hostel, but this was not as liberal as it seemed. The prescribed visiting hours were between 2.00 pm and 4.00 pm on Saturday and Sunday afternoons. Long enough, you might think, but girl-friends were only allowed in the public lounge, not students' rooms, unless you both had your parents' permission – in writing – for that specific visit. These 'deterrents' were simply circumvented – you just took the girls up to your room and socialised, risking being chucked out. Several promising teaching careers ended this way, with pregnancies and expulsions. The pill was yet to come.

There was an awful lot of fairly harmless fun. Hostel Five was notorious for practical jokes. When my friend asked me to his room for a coffee, the door fell into the room as he opened it, as someone had removed the hinges! When the only first year student on their floor told the gang that he was taking his girl-friend to his room on a Saturday afternoon, he took her upstairs, and entered a room devoid of everything, and was compelled to entertain her in the lounge. The fun just went on and on.

Padgate's motto was impressive: "Sagax Semper Discit" ("The wise man is always learning"). The curriculum was no challenge and some of it even interested me, but

A College brochure showing the new residential blocks, as well as students attending assembly and presentation ceremonies and performing a play, 1956.

what I learned at Padgate was to educate myself. I learned to love reading. My main subject was Chemistry, but I read all my mate's set books for English, and another close friend's History and Social Studies texts. Then I discovered Freud and got interested in Psychology – which later stood me in good stead.

I was also catching up on the Arts side. I went to classical concerts and learned to play the guitar. I also discovered jazz and heard Duke Ellington at the Free Trade Hall. There was a tradition that the Second Years put on a welcoming concert for the new First Years early in the Autumn Term. I was quite smitten when Iola Parry sang "Velia!" The First Years had to reply by Christmas. I got heavily involved and the sketches became the Rag Show that travelled South-East Lancashire the following summer.

But it was not all fun. When I found myself at Winton County Secondary School for Boys, six weeks into College, untrained and thrown to the lions, I was ready to leave. Miss Barker, our Hostel Warden, told me that everyone went through this and she had wanted to quit too, at that stage. I stuck with it, and by the third year was actually enjoying some of my teaching practice. In my view, anyone who can survive 5B for RE on a Friday afternoon is capable of holding down any job in the world! I did not stay in school teaching – my wife and I now run a management training company – but I suppose I have been a teacher all my life.

Some of my friends are disparaging about Padgate, but for me it was the opportunity of a lifetime, and I have not a moment of regret that I "served" three years there. I loved all my "cells", my "cell-mates" became friends for life, and some of the "warders" were fun people, too.

Joyce Martin retired in 1963 after 14 years as Principal. She was a kind, caring and considerate woman, who inspired the best from people. She gave chances to students who did not quite fit the criteria for other colleges, if she believed they would make good teachers. Her strong judge of character did not often fail her. Above all, she had a sense of humour. She was greatly admired by her colleagues, students and friends worldwide, made through her membership of Soroptimists International. Dr J. Lance Dobson, MA, MEd, PhD, succeeded her. The following year, members of the Old Students' Association presented her with a portrait painted by a tutor, Mr Mount. She accepted it and asked that it remain in College. Dr Dobson requested that it be hung in Martin Hall (Hall Three), until the new Assembly Hall was completed.

John Williams, Dr Lance Dobson, Betty Moisley and Bill Buckley unveiling a plaque commemorating Joyce Martin, the founder Principal of Padgate College.

Between 1962 and 1966, large-scale building work was carried out in two phases, in order to bring the College up to date, to improve provision for the accommodation and teaching needs of the students, and to provide suitable administration facilities. Following the earlier building of the halls of residence, work for the first phase concentrated on the tutorial needs. A three-storey Tutorial Building, which included a Library and Students' Common Room, was erected. A detached Gymnasium Block and new entrances were also included. The next phase of building works created another three-storey Science Block that was added as an extension to the Tutorial Building, together with a Rural Science Wing, and a single-storey Music Block. A new Administration Centre was also built, with a Main Entrance Hall, a Kitchen and a Dining Hall. A two-storey Sick Bay and Domestic Staff Building completed the scheme. These teaching and administration facilities were situated to the northern side of the campus, near Crab Lane.

Goronwy Roberts, MP, Minister of State for Education and Science, officially opened these extensions to Padgate College of Education on the 2nd June 1967. The programme for the event shows that at that time Cuthbert Myers and Margaret Julier were the Deputy Principals, and the tutorial staff totalled 82. County Alderman J. Selwyn Jones was Chairman of Governors. Twelve of the 17 Governors were either County Aldermen or County Councillors.

The Students' Common Room (Tutorial Block); taken from the programme for the official opening of the Padgate College extension, June 1967.

The University of Manchester had instituted a four year course of study leading to the awarding of a BEd degree. The first cohort of students to complete the course graduated in 1969.

During the 1960s, there was a period when student unrest was rampant at colleges and universities throughout the country. This unrest was absent from Padgate, for students had achieved what they wanted peacefully, thanks to the wise guidance of Dr Dobson. Andy Slater was President of the Students' Union at the time, and gives a clear picture of these developments:

In 1968, when every university and college in England (and Europe) seemed to be on strike, here at Padgate we had excellent relations with the College Authorities. Student representation was being built up as a result of our meetings with Dr Dobson and through the Staff-Student Consultation Committees in all subject areas. These later went on to ensure full student representations on the Governing Body. Dr Dobson was instrumental in setting these up and in developing a sense of student responsibility and democracy within the College.

Dr Dobson did a great deal for students at this time; mainly, I believe, as a result of the good working relations between the Students' Union, himself and his Senior Management Team. I know for a fact that many of his "concessions" (I would refer to them as "sensible and realistic changes") were opposed by many of the more conservative tutors. These included much more liberal visiting hours in the halls of residence; better kitchen facilities in all halls; TVs in some lounges; the use of College mini buses by the Union and societies; doubling-up some rooms to cater for as many students as possible in 'Halls'; allowing us to bring a bank to College and providing a room for it; and not least for allowing us to collect three years' Union subscriptions for all students. Dr Dobson was indeed very supportive of everything the SU tried to do. He never said "No" to any of our requests without first giving it a great deal of thought. He once remarked: "Wise people always think what they say before they say it."

I learned a lot from Dr Dobson, who I regarded as one of the leaders in the democratisation of student politics. Indeed, it was his own suggestion that my successor should be granted a full sabbatical year to act as President. This really was unusual for a College of our size. It was actions from people like him that helped greatly in getting Parliament to lower the age of responsibility from 21 to 18 only a few years after I left Padgate.

Dr Dobson himself believed that his time as Principal coincided with a period of growth and development at the College, highlighted by the increase in student numbers. Dr Dobson was a strong supporter of the Old Students' Association, encouraging their activities, and attending Reunions with his wife. He was held in high esteem.

A FAMILY POINT OF VIEW...

Obviously, most of the history of Padgate so far has come from written records or personal memories of former students. There were, of course, others who saw and experienced things from a different perspective. Staff members see things *in loco parentis*, from the teachers' point of view. Helen Henwood, née Dobson, provided this overview of Padgate as experienced by a family member:

I moved to live at Padgate College of Education in April 1963, when my father, Dr Lance Dobson, was appointed as Principal. On reflection, it was a time when rapid change was in the air – political, social, cultural and educational – and so it was on the cusp of this change, which was reflected in the way Padgate subsequently developed and evolved, that we moved from Newcastle upon Tyne. I was 14 then and this was my first move. It was a very different way of life from that which I had known, lived much more in the public eye, with all the constraints which that brings. My father was wholly committed to his work at Padgate – and was extremely professional. Yet that also meant that work and home life were dovetailed together – a sort of living over the shop – which was not easy for a teenager! We lived at the end of a row of modern terraced houses, College Close, from where you could see lots of activity on the campus, just as we were visible too, I expect. At the time the campus was quite open – there were newly planted saplings, which of course have grown to maturity now, 40 years later, making it a very leafy campus by comparison.

The campus was then a combination of the older, low-level wartime buildings and the newer, distinctive halls of residence; the main offices were at that time still in the old buildings, and the new offices were not built until a few years later. The first summer we were there, I remember going to an Open Day, when there were a lot of exhibitions and displays and the College was looking at its best. The Art Department had some new and exciting modern art on display, and the Drama and Music Departments put on a full-length joint production of 'The Threepenny Opera'. This collaboration between Kurt Weill and Bertolt Brecht is not an easy work to stage and yet it was absolutely stunning – very polished and professional. I was so impressed, I saw it three times! I went to College dances. Initially it tended to be trad jazz – Monty Sunshine, even Johnny Dankworth and Cleo Laine once – but later, in the wake of the rapid change in popular music, more rock and roll, blues and soul, including Padgate's very own King Bees (who did a great rendition of "Smokestack Lightning!")

My father regularly had meetings with the Students' Council in our house, or with visitors from other colleges or from the University of Manchester. Visitors from further afield came to stay overnight and so it was always very busy at home, and my mother produced wonderful meals – fortunately, she enjoyed cooking!

Both my parents greatly enjoyed their nine years at Padgate until my father's retirement in 1972, and looked back on their time there with great affection. I was at school in Warrington for four years until I left home in 1967, to go to London to train as a teacher myself. Then Padgate was still semi-rural, on the outskirts of Warrington. Now it is surrounded by extensive development. Much as these things have changed, so has the status of Padgate in its several incarnations. Yet it retains something of its original atmosphere and it is that which keeps old students and others like myself loyal to it, interested in its progress, and happy to celebrate its history.

CROSSING THE BORDER...

Dr Dobson retired in April 1972 and was succeeded by John Williams, MA. Mr Williams had hardly taken up his post when rumbles of closure threatened the College.

Teacher training was being reduced and many well known training colleges were in the same position. The Old Students' Association joined forces with the College and other interested parties in the fight for survival. Eventually, the threat of closure was lifted. Mike Hall, MP, and his wife Lesley (née Gosling) were students at Padgate at the time of unrest. They both recollect how at the time there were few teaching jobs and mass unemployment, and how students occupied the academic buildings for accommodation, some even sleeping under the tutors' desks.

Diversification into non-teaching areas such as Media Studies, Drama and Sports Studies was essential to maintain the life of the College. Further Education courses were provided, alongside the Higher Education subjects. In 1974, government boundary changes moved Warrington from Lancashire into Cheshire, much to the disgust of many Lancastrians and indeed many from other parts of the country who knew Padgate as part of Lancashire. The name plaque was removed from the wall by the entrance and stored until a suitable site could be found for it.

In 1975, Padgate was validated to offer BA Humanities degrees as well as teacher training (BEd degrees and Post-Graduate Certificates in Education).

TIMES OF CHANGE...

In 1979, the College became a constituent part of the new North Cheshire College, merging with the former Art College and the Technical College in Warrington. A service to mark the end of Padgate College of Higher Education as a separate institution was held at Padgate Parish Church on the 22nd June, 1978. The Revd E. Wickham, Bishop of Middleton, was the preacher. Old Students' Association members who attended were dismayed that no mention was made of Miss Martin's long service as founder Principal for 14 years. The Vicar promised to include prayers for her during the following Sunday services. The College produced a range of commemorative plates, mugs and tiles for sale, each bearing the College crest and appropriate dates.

With the merger of the colleges, John Williams, the Principal, and Margaret Julier, Vice-Principal, retired. William Buckley, OBE, BSc (Hons) (Eng), MEd, CEng,

FIMechE, FRSA, FBIM, became Director of the North Cheshire College, spending time at both Padgate and Warrington. He was also a member of the Council of the University of Manchester. There was a need to continue developing the curriculum. During this time, subjects such as Media Studies and Drama came to the fore. With all its changes and innovations, there was a deep concern within the College that Higher Education had to be present, maintained and cultivated.

New teacher training admissions ceased from 1983, and teacher training was finally wound up by 1987.

Mr Buckley retired in 1987, and was replaced by Dr Terry Keen. This was a period of change. Out went the traditional College colours, to be replaced by lighter shades, as shown on *The Clothes Show*, a popular Sunday afternoon TV fashion programme of the day. Commercial activities were undertaken because of a financial short-fall. The academic staff totalled 245. Yet, in spite of all the changes, much of the old tradition remained. Following Dr Keen's departure for a college in the South-West of England, Mr D. Pride became Director, and served until his retirement in 1993. Dr Alan Smith took over as interim Principal during a year in which the next Principal was sought.

In the same year, the College changed its title yet again, and became the Padgate Campus of Warrington Collegiate Institute. The other sites were the former Technical College in Winwick Road and the Art College in Museum Street, Warrington. In 1994, Steven Broomhead, MA, became Principal. Courses continued to develop, and HE student numbers grew, with Hilary Tucker as Dean of Higher Education. By 1995, there were 883 full-time students, and the Buckley Suite became a training restaurant.

LOOKING BACK…

Dr Alan Smith retired in 1994, having been a member of staff since 1963, in a number of roles. He provided this account:

I joined the staff of Padgate Training College in May 1963, as a very junior lecturer in Geography. In fact, I was the first new member of staff to be appointed by the then new Principal, Dr Lance Dobson. Little did I imagine at the time that I would stay for 32 years, leaving in April 1994 as Principal myself.

Padgate in 1963 was small, intimate and comfortable. Students knew one another, staff had time to teach and interact with students, and above everything the College knew what it was about and where it was going. It was a time of expansion and optimism, under the strong leadership of Dr Lance Dobson and later John Williams. Building workers from Seddon were permanently on site, as one new building after another was completed – dining halls, Gymnasium and old teaching blocks were gradually replaced. The "founding fathers" (Myers, Barker, Wood, Gregory, Aitcheson, Walters, Peach, Sconce, Birch, Gooch, and Thomas) were joined by the increasing band of newer, younger staff. New subjects were appearing on the curriculum – Sociology, Languages, American Studies, even CCTV. These were lively times; the College had responded to the national need for more teachers and was a major player in the North-West region.

The 1970s saw many changes and challenges. The advent of the BA degree courses and the one year PGCE brought different students and the diversification of our courses and outlooks. The eventual loss of Initial Teacher Training was a major blow, and a catalyst for enormous changes and the radical reshaping of the College. We had come to a point which we would revisit frequently – "when in trouble - restructure". With the advantage of hindsight, I can reflect that I was one of the fortunate ones. Growth up to the end of the 1970s had brought promotion. Change, however, for many staff colleagues meant demotivation, disillusionment, moves of career, premature retirement and changes they could not cope with.

'North Cheshire College', the new name adopted in 1979, was thought by many to be rather bland and somewhat meaningless, but the change marked a real turning-point for some people. My recollection of the 1980s is one of constant change and readjustment – more "restructuring" and the advent of "management" into all our vocabularies. The emergence of this new, larger, amalgamated College seemed right at the time, with good reasons behind it. Time, however, demonstrated it was an uneasy and unsustainable arrangement. The bold move of starting afresh with Higher Education provision proved right in the long run, and its roots have evolved into the present provision within the new University. I am proud to be associated with what became known as "The New Degree Project". Our continued association with the University of Manchester was an aspect of my work I found stimulating. The new Joint Honours degree programmes in Media, Leisure and Recreation and associated Business and IT courses became a success, and hopefully past students now look back on them as springboards to highly successful careers.

I look back on 32 happy, eventful and satisfying years. Padgate gave me many opportunities, at times some headaches. I made many lasting friendships, for which I am eternally grateful. During my time, Padgate had five different titles. I worked for five Principals, all of remarkably different outlooks and persuasions. I had nine different job titles; perhaps this was the way to survive or I may have just stayed too long. I was pleased to hear of the developments on site, and particularly pleased to hear that investment had become possible. For much of the 1980s and early 1990s, we always seemed to be in a position of making do with what we had in terms of both human and physical resources. I wish the new University success in the future and Padgate at least another 60 years of continuing to serve the educational needs of successive generations.

In 1996, the College celebrated its Golden Jubilee. Past students contributed to a commemorative exhibition. During that year's Annual Reunion, which was well attended, members of the Old Students' Association made a video – *Memories of Padgate: 1946-1996*. Former students - ranging from members of the Experienced Teachers' Course to newer members, and also Dr Dobson, spoke of their particular memories of their time at Padgate. The day's events ended with a magnificent firework display, provided by the College.

The following year, Steven Broomhead resigned from the College to take up a new post as Chief Executive of Warrington Unitary Authority. Hilary Tucker, MLitt, BA, TCert, Dean of Higher Education for several years and then Deputy Principal, was appointed to replace him.

Dr Dobson died in April 1999. Mike Owen, a former Lecturer during Dr Dobson's time as Principal, spoke of a warm man with a sense of humour – one who had done much to ensure the future growth of the College. Dr Dobson himself had expressed his own appreciation of the warmth and friendship of his many friends at Padgate, and of his particular affection for the Old Students' Association, whose members had welcomed him as President and then into membership following his retirement.

In September 1999, past and current staff from the Geography Department, together with members of his family, attended the unveiling of a memorial to Stan Wood, who had been Principal Lecturer in Geography from 1946 to 1968. It took the form of an armillary sphere mounted on a plinth. College had provided a secure, open and sunny quad between the Sports Hall and the Teaching Block to display it. Stan Wood was much loved and respected by the former students he had taught, or who had been in his Personal Groups. He had continued to attend Reunions right up to the year before his death. He was well known for his endless fund of funny stories, with which he regaled any group of people he met, and was also highly regarded by all those who knew him.

FLUCTUATIONS...

In 1986, the Higher Education numbers on the Padgate campus had fallen to 270; over the next six years they increased to 750. The most successful period, number-wise, occurred in the mid-1990s, when permission was granted for the Higher Education faculty to be called "University College Warrington". The title was bestowed on the College for its high quality by the University of Manchester, and was initially supported by the incoming Labour Government. However, following the recommendations of the Dearing Report in 1997, legislation was introduced which required a number of institutions to relinquish the title of 'University College', among them University College Warrington.

APPROACHING GRADUATION...

2002 brought major changes to the structure of the entire College. Hilary Tucker, as Principal, felt that developments in Higher and Further Education nationally were pointing to a new form of organisation for the College. It was clear to her that for Padgate to maintain and develop Higher Education in Warrington, it needed to become fully part of a larger Higher Education Institution. It could then access the capital investment needed for Higher Education to grow on the Padgate campus.

With the support of the Governors of the College, Hilary Tucker negotiated the

Mike Owen, Dr Alan Smith and other members of the Geography Department unveiling the armillary sphere, a memorial to Stan Wood.

merger of the Higher Education College at Padgate campus with Chester College of Higher Education, which was to revert to the name 'University College Chester' in 2003, when it was granted Taught Degree Awarding Powers [TDAP]. In addition, she gained approval and funding support for a complete new build of the Winwick Road campus for Further Education – the new Warrington Collegiate. These were Hilary's final achievements before she retired on the 31st August 2002, after 27 years at the College. She is now a member of the Council of the new University of Chester, still supporting Padgate. Warrington Town Council, long-time supporter of Padgate and its activities, was very supportive of the initiative. Chester College of Higher Education, planning to apply for full university status once it had been granted TDAP, would have space to expand in a town that already had a history of appreciation for education.

Chester College of Higher Education was a particularly appropriate institution for the Higher Education College at Padgate to merge with, as Warrington was associated with the founding of the original teacher training college at Chester in 1840. Horatio Powys, Rector of Warrington, was one of the six founders of Chester Teacher Training College, and one of the instrumental meetings that led to the foundation of Chester College was held in the Warrington National School building. Also, although it was founded by the Church of England, Chester had for most of its long history been a similar institution to Padgate, until it expanded very rapidly in the 1990s, particularly with the development of courses in Nursing and Midwifery and the founding of the Chester Business School.

The merger between the Higher Education College at Padgate and Chester College of Higher Education was not a speedy process. The many legal and financial implications associated with the merger of two organisations meant that a year's preparation was necessary before it could take place. The merger was ratified on the 1st August 2002, under the guidance of Dr Malcolm Rhodes, project manager, who was Dean of Higher Education at Padgate at the time. When the merger was in process it was essential for Dr Rhodes, now Pro-Vice-Chancellor of the University of Chester, to seek external funding so that the capital projects on the Padgate campus could be undertaken. The Padgate site, to be known from that time as the Warrington campus, received a £4 million grant from the Higher Education Funding Council for England [HEFCE], as well as £2.4 million from the Northwest Regional Development Agency [NWDA]. Overall, a sum in the region of £10-12 million was designated for capital investment on the Warrington campus, provided through external grants and by Chester College of Higher Education. Now that the money for capital investment had been secured, the redevelopment programme on the Warrington campus could begin.

Being part of Chester College of Higher Education gave Padgate a new identity and projected a sense of excitement and anticipation. Significant progress was soon apparent across the campus, as the first phase of the redevelopment programme began. An all-weather floodlit sports facility was established, windows in the Lance Dobson Hall were replaced, and a landscaping project for the Warrington campus was undertaken. The old bistro was also completely redesigned into two sections, refurbished and given new names, the "Garden Dining Room" and the "Terrace Bar Café". As well as these projects, various painting, recarpeting and general maintenance programmes were commenced on the site.

The merger with Chester College of Higher Education also led to many academic changes, as well as physical developments on the Padgate campus. The control of academic departments was assimilated with those at the Chester campus and departments that were previously being run locally on the Padgate site were now being managed from Chester. In 2003, Teacher Education programmes returned to the Padgate campus, shortly followed by the Nurse Training provision that had previously been based at Warrington Hospital. Social Work programmes are perhaps the best example of academic growth on the Warrington campus since the merger with Chester College of Higher Education. A course for roughly thirty students has grown to provision for a full range of degrees, and teaching of the subject at Padgate is now rated as among the best in the country.

Students and teachers at the Warrington campus took advantage of the many personal opportunities created by the merger with Chester College of Higher Education. Students benefited, as they now had a wider choice of courses to choose from and increased access to learning resources. They also benefited from the increased range of facilities on offer through the developments on the Warrington campus, along with new access to those at Chester. Staff members had the experience of working in a university environment and took full advantage of the opportunities available for further professional education and promotion. A member of staff at the time,

Karen Willis, recalls how the change brought a big identity change for the Padgate campus and increased career possibilities for staff members. Since the merger project, Karen became consecutively Academic Quality and Standards Manager, Learning and Teaching Institute Manager and now Director of Widening Access.

While the building work was easily seen and progress could be followed, a massive undertaking was continuing back in Chester, as the College produced the mass of evidence required in order to fulfil the requirements for University status. Finally, on the 21st March 2005 the College received the news that it had waited for – full University status had been granted. From the 1st August 2005, the new title of the former Padgate College would be the University of Chester, Warrington campus. New sign-boards, new titles, designs for the various gowns, and plans for the official ceremonies all required urgent attention. His Grace the Duke of Westminster became the Chancellor of the new University, and Professor Tim Wheeler the Vice-Chancellor. The splendid Inauguration Ceremony took place in Chester Cathedral. The University was launched in Warrington on Monday, the 19th September 2005, with a lunch on the campus. The chief guest was the Mayor of Warrington, who unveiled a plaque in the Refectory in the presence of the Mayoress, other civic dignitaries and guests.

Between Easter 2004 and February 2006, the second phase of the redevelopment programme was undertaken on the Warrington campus. The Derek Newton Theatre was refurbished and renamed the North-West Media Centre. Blatchford Hall was also refurbished and reconfigured to allow the University's Nurse Training provision at Warrington to be relocated from the Hospital. A new Students' Union Office and Administration Centre were placed in the main building. As well as this, the Students' Union itself, with new sports changing facilities, was relocated to the refurbished and reconfigured Buckley Suite. The completion of the demolition programme on campus, removing all remaining wartime buildings, concluded the second phase of the Warrington campus redevelopment programme.

Plans were made to celebrate the 60th anniversary of the Padgate campus at the Old Students' Reunion in 2006. A guest list was drawn up, beginning with the Mayor of Warrington, and including as many of the former Principals and Directors as could be tracked down, as well as Colin Daniels, the former Chair of Governors, and Mike Hall, a former student and currently a local Member of Parliament.

Developments on the Padgate site are still taking place as student numbers increase. Phase Three of the redevelopment programme is now underway, with a new Business and IT building being constructed and an extension to the Learning Resources Centre being undertaken. The new buildings were scheduled for completion by August 2007 and will be fully operational for students and staff by September 2007. In keeping with the tradition of the Padgate campus, the new buildings recall former staff members. The Business and IT Centre will acknowledge the former Principal Hilary Tucker, whilst the Learning Resources building will be renamed after another former Principal, Steven Broomhead. The construction of these buildings outlines the continuing growth and success on the Padgate campus.

Ben Barrett was a student on the Padgate campus from 2003 until 2006 and is now Students' Union Vice-President for Warrington. He remembers witnessing a time of advancement at Padgate:

Betty Moisley, founder member and Vice-President of POSA and Cllr Mrs Linda Dirir, Mayor of Warrington, cut the 60th Anniversary cake at the Reunion on the 9th September, 2006.

The first time I visited Padgate campus, I could tell that this would be the place where I would be earning my degree; a somewhat small place, but strangely it felt like home. Even now, when I look back on my first arrival, it still brings a smile to my face. I am not alone in this as many former "Freshers" have also experienced this phenomenon. Even people who have left start smiling as soon as you mention the campus. There is something about this campus, although no one is sure what it is. All we do know is that many people have different memories, but mainly what they all have in common is that these are fond memories of the place.

I have been residing on the campus now for almost four years and in that time I have seen so much of the campus change, mainly for the better, and improve for the students. Let me take you back to my first September, in 2003.

What surprised me when I first arrived was the fact that the campus was split into three sections: the first was used by University College Chester; the second was the new

Warrington Collegiate Institute, which is now a Further Education College based mainly in the town: and lastly the campus was used as the North-West Training Centre for the police service. All of the old buildings were in use; the H Block, the Derek Newton Theatre and of course the old bar and bunker. This year was the first year during which improvements on the campus were scheduled, and a lot happened within a short time. The improvements included a new bistro, repair works to the Derek Newton Theatre, and demolition of the H Block. The first thing, however, was the removal of the other occupants from the campus.

This happened towards the end of my first year of study; both the Collegiate and the police force left the campus, leaving only the University College students. Once this happened, the University College could then start work on the promised improvements. The old bistro was demolished and slowly rebuilt over the next academic year. The building work also began on structurally stabilising the Derek Newton Theatre, which again was a lengthy process, as it was a listed building. During these building works, it was decided that the H Block would also be demolished to allow for future expansion, which has just begun.

Whilst the new bistro was being built, the old Buckley Suite was used during most of my second year. Because of work on the Derek Newton Theatre, the Performing Arts students were relocated in and around the campus. Work also began on refurbishing the Conference Centre, so that it would have en suite facilities for the following year.

At the end of my second year, the new bistro was completed and was warmly received by students and staff. With the completion of the new bistro, it was decided that the Buckley Suite would be converted into a new bar for the campus, as the old one was becoming more dangerous and in desperate need of repair. So work began on the new bar building. The Derek Newton Theatre was also eventually finished, with the outer shell of the building being reinforced, which made it more secure and preserved the theatre for the future.

In January 2006, the student bar was finished and renamed the Friendly Union [FU] Bar. This now provides a new environment for the Students' Union to entertain the students. With the opening of the new bar, the old one could be demolished safely. This process was prolonged because of asbestos in the ceiling. A group of students and staff watched the beginning of the demolition, bringing a sad end to such a great building, which had so many memories for so many generations of students dating back to the 1960s.

The final year of my course saw no new building work, which brought a welcome change, as we could make use of all the facilities on the campus without much disruption. However, there was a demolition of one small house at the end of the campus where the former senior residential tutor had been based. This was knocked down to create additional parking space for the ever increasing number of Nursing students.

Although I graduated last year with a degree in Performing Arts and Media, I was voted in to run the Students' Union for a year. So I got to stay on the campus and live the student life that little bit longer. This year has seen a big increase, not only in student numbers, but also in building work. Our Learning Resources Centre is being extended and will be three times the size of the original building. This has been welcomed by students and staff, as now key texts/journals and additional resources will be more easily accessible.

The University has also begun work on a new Business and IT Centre, which will allow the Business School to operate within its own space to teach its degree programmes; it will also incorporate an open IT suite for students to access computers 24 hours a day. There are plans for an additional road to be laid running alongside the new Centre, making access easier from the main road.

The final plan for this year is to create new parking spaces, a new road within the campus and make the "Piazza" more pedestrian friendly. Also, resurfacing of many roads is to be undertaken.

All this work is scheduled for completion by September 2007, when the new intake of students will arrive on the campus. Every year, it seems, something has changed on this campus, but the spirit of it still survives. This is exemplified by the Padgate Old Student Association [POSA], which visits the campus around three times a year and traditionally holds an Annual Reunion there. We arrange for current students to lead tours of the campus, and both old and new students share their experiences and recall the fun times they have had at Padgate.

All the building work that has been done in the past four years has benefited everyone who uses the campus on a daily basis. Although some of the old character may have been lost and buildings that had so many fond memories attached to them are gone, those who have lived on or visited the Padgate campus know that it is still a special place and I hope it always will be.

PADGATE OLD STUDENTS' ASSOCIATION

On the 13th September 1949, the first of the two year teacher training students arrived. During the next seven months, members of both the "Experienced Teachers" intake and the new students worked together and made friendships. Before the Experienced Teachers' Group left Padgate, Miss Martin suggested that they should hold a reunion. One of their number, Betty Moisley, had the foresight to collect one shilling (5 p.) and a home address from everyone who wished to remain in contact. The first ever Padgate Reunion was held during the weekend of the 1st October 1950. It was deemed a success – especially the formal Dinner on the Saturday evening, for which long frocks were worn. In 1951, the first two year students attended a reunion. As further course members joined, it became necessary to form a Committee to organise the activities. Two representatives were elected from each year group. In 1953, a Constitution was drawn up, office-holders were elected and so Padgate Old Students' Association (soon known to everyone as POSA) came into being. The aims were to enable former students to keep in touch with each other, and to meet socially; to distribute information on matters of common interest to past and present students; and to preserve among former students an interest in the continuing life and work of the College.

In May 1953, POSA appointed a magazine sub-editor for *POSA News*. Thereafter, a large section of the magazine was devoted to the activities of the Association, and individual course representatives gave details provided by their members. It was avidly read by former students, eager to maintain contact with the College and with each other.

At this time, Padgate Old Students' Association Reunions were held over the Whitsuntide weekend, with a wide range of activities. As well as the Committee Meeting and Annual General Meeting, there was a chapel service, a sherry reception and a formal dinner. Feature films, music or record recitals, table tennis tournaments, tennis and country dancing all appeared on early programmes. Coach trips were also tried, but were not popular. It was the job of the most recent leavers to clear the tables and do the washing up after the dinner.

In 1959, POSA joined the celebrations of the 10th Anniversary of the College during its weekend Reunion. A fund had been opened to provide new gates for the Main Entrance to the College, and the Association was invited to contribute. Members preferred to pay instead for a quality name plaque to replace the board bearing the College name, which was to be situated by the gate. The red rose of Lancashire was featured.

In 1966, the Old Students' Association made the first K. M. Herring Award to the student of Art & Design who had made the most progress during his/her course. It was made in honour of Kay Herring, Craft Tutor and a fine artist in her own right, who had died following a serious illness. She was much admired and respected. POSA members donated funds in her memory to set up the Annual Award.

Old Students' Annual Reunions had always previously been held over a weekend. In 1967, however, the first one day Reunion was held, during which members joined in the celebrations for the 21st Anniversary of the opening of Padgate.

Following the death in retirement of C. J. H. Myers, a former Art Tutor and Vice-Principal, POSA paid for the Memorial Rose Garden situated beside the cafeteria, and for a garden bench. College paid for a wall, and the Myers family presented a birdbath. Mr Myers's family attended the 1978 Reunion for the installation. The members of the 1952-54 Course wished to mark the 25th Anniversary of the start of their course by donating a crab apple tree to the College. This was also planted in the garden. The original intention was not only to honour Mr Myers, but also to provide a reminder of the foundation of the College by Lancashire County Council. The old College name plaque with the red rose was to have been mounted on the wall behind the garden, but unfortunately this was found not to be strong enough, so it was put into storage again until a suitable place could be found.

In November 1979, those who had known her were saddened to learn of the death of Joyce Martin. POSA immediately opened a memorial fund, with the strong support of past and present tutors. A legacy from Miss Martin was left to POSA, with the proviso that it be used for the benefit of past and present students. With the agreement of College, a memorial plaque was mounted in the entrance foyer, and a garden seat was placed in the Memorial Rose Garden. The remaining money was invested to provide an annual award to students.

During 2000, Margaret Julier returned to the College to unveil the memorial plaque to Dr Dobson, in the presence of his family. The plaque was situated beside the Hall that bore his name. This was the College's gift. Helen Henwood, his daughter, who had herself lived on the site as a youngster, expressed the family's gratitude at the honour shown to her father's memory. POSA members decided to make a perpetual award to the student chosen by the student body as having done most for his/her peers. A glass salver in the old College colours of red, white and black was chosen. The recipient each year also receives a cheque.

EVER CONSTANT...

Throughout the growth and development of Higher Education on the Padgate site, one constant has remained – the Padgate Old Students' Association, which still continues its work today. Betty Moisley, a member of the original Experienced Teachers' Group, was a member of the Executive Committee throughout, until her sad death in January 2007. One aim of the Association is to enable students to remain in contact with each other and with the College. This is done principally through the Annual Reunion, which includes on its agenda the Annual General Meeting of the Association.

Each Principal or Director of the College has been invited to become President of the Association, and all have accepted. Earlier Presidents lived on site and were able to take a very active role. In recent years, additional duties and calls on their time for professional reasons have limited the activities of some Presidents to some extent. However great or small the participation, the link is vital and members have always been appreciative of this co-operation. Both Joyce Martin and Dr Lance Dobson maintained membership and attended Reunions throughout their retirement, until prevented by ill health. Bill Buckley also retained his membership, and remains an active Committee member and Vice-President of the Association. Hilary Tucker had been a hardworking member of the Committee during the time she was Dean, College Deputy Principal and, as Principal, President of POSA. She was made an Honorary Vice-President upon her retirement.

The POSA Constitution provides for staff membership, and there are places for staff and ex-tutors on the Committee. Throughout the years, the Association has been well served by tutors and ex-tutors, who have maintained support for the Association and its activities. Stan Wood and Dorothy Peach continued their practical support until shortly before their deaths. Phil Lloyd, Derrick Bowden and David Grimshaw served as Treasurers of the Joyce Martin Fund. Mike Owen was the Association Treasurer at the time of his final illness. Tutors and ex-tutors continue actively working today. Bernard Boyes is another ex-tutor who devotes time to the Association as a very active

Vice-President. Our thanks are owed to these and to many other staff members who have contributed in other ways.

A second aim was support for current students in College. This continued with the annual presentation of awards. The K. M. Herring Award was founded for students in the Art and Design Department who had shown the greatest development in their skills. Several award winners went on to further their artistic education at university or art college. Winners have been chosen, not only from the fine arts field, but also from other specialised areas, such as silversmithing and more recently web design. Award winners have used the cheques they received to purchase materials, books or to visit particular exhibitions.

The Joyce Martin Award has been used for the benefit of many students in a variety of situations. Support has been given, for example, to expeditions to the Atlas Mountains and to the Faeroe Isles. Grants have been given to groups performing on the Edinburgh Festival Fringe, and to individual students working in education in the Czech Republic. Sports teams have been supported and trophies provided for Inter-College competitions. One student was given a grant to help him get to the Paralympic Games in Seoul. In recent years, calls for this kind of support have been less frequent. The Award is therefore now made to the Highest Achiever. This was done to bring the College into line with others attached to the University of Manchester.

The latest award for students is the J. L. Dobson Trophy. This is awarded to the student judged by the student body to have done most to support his/her peers. The Trophy is kept in the College, but winners receive a cheque. All three awards are reserved for students from the Warrington campus.

The Executive Committee has again co-opted members of the Students' Union of the Warrington campus to serve on the Committee. This forms a valuable and close two-way link between past and present students, to enable us to fulfil our aim better. It would also have pleased Joyce Martin.

When Padgate became associated with Chester College of Higher Education, David Hughes, the Registrar of the Chester College Old Students' Association, was invited to join the Committee. In return, Elsie Newton, POSA Secretary, was co-opted to join the Chester Executive Committee. A first step was thus taken in forming a link between the two alumni groups. David Marshall, the Director of Corporate Communications in Chester, became a staff member. When he left the University shortly afterwards, Jayne Dodgson replaced him. All the Committee Members had expertise that benefited POSA and encouraged its work. In 2006, the Committee warmly welcomed Dorothy Marriss, Deputy Vice-Chancellor, to the Committee. She now has particular responsibility for the Warrington campus, and represents Professor Wheeler at POSA meetings and events.

POSA was instrumental in the setting up of the Padgate Memorial Garden. A tour of the grounds will reveal, not only the armorial sphere, but also a number of benches where students and visitors alike can rest for a while and enjoy the pleasant surroundings. The plaques on these benches show that they were bought by old students in memory of former tutors. The tutors probably would not recognise the campus now, but would be pleased to see that it is still home to a thriving student population.

Hilary Tucker, Dorothy Bradbury and Bill Buckley presenting the Joyce Martin Award to a recent recipient.

The Association Committee has also begun to establish a Padgate Archive in the Board Room, with memorabilia donated by members, together with the Minute Books of the Association. It is important that this heritage is neither lost nor forgotten. Further additions will be accepted, as we seek to develop this area of our work.

POSA COMMITTEE 2006.

PRESIDENT - Professor Timothy Wheeler, DL. (Vice-Chancellor)

HONORARY VICE-PRESIDENT - Hilary Tucker. (Ex-Principal)

VICE-PRESIDENT - William E. Buckley, OBE. (Ex-Director)

VICE-PRESIDENT- Betty Moisley. (Experienced Teachers' Group)

VICE-PRESIDENT - Bernard Boyes. (Ex-Tutor)

VICE-PRESIDENT - Dorothy Bradbury. (1955-57)

VICE-PRESIDENT AND SECRETARY - Elsie Newton. (1954-56)

TREASURER - Curtis McFarlane.

JOYCE MARTIN FUND TREASURER - David Grimshaw. (Staff)

Phyllis Custerson. (1952-54)

Ada Temperley. (1954-56)

Tanya Eastwood. (1955-58)

Brenda Lee. (1956-58)

Andrew Slater. (1966-69)

Jennifer Fisher. (1967-71)

Ian Glover. (1967-70)

David McGealy. (1967-71)

Ian Rice. (1967-71)

Margaret Westgarth. (1969-72)

Helene Craig. (1983-86)

Jackie Timmis. (1972-75)

Dr Malcolm Rhodes. (Pro-Vice-Chancellor)

Dorothy Marriss. (Deputy Vice-Chancellor)

David Hughes. (Alumni Registrar, Chester)

Jayne Dodgson. (Director of Corporate Communications)

Anne Cooper. (1972-75)

Jenny Brown. (1972-75)

Ben Barrett. (Students' Union Vice-President)

Liam O'Sullivan. (Students' Union Academic Officer)

Dan Mills. (Students' Union Council Chair)

EPILOGUE...

When, in 2005, the Committee first discussed suggestions for celebrating the 60th Anniversary of the site, Ian Rice suggested that a commemorative booklet could be written that outlined the development of Higher Education at Padgate. Professor Wheeler thought that this was a good idea and should be possible. So to him we owe the impetus to set the wheels in motion.

The only problem was where to find the relevant information, and how to get everything done in such a short time. POSA members had contributed items to an exhibition several years ago, and it was thought that a College archive was going to be built up. We also knew that at one time Derek Newton was writing a history of the College but, after he died, no one knew where to find his notes or archive material. Eventually, some items were found in a lecture room and made their way to the Board Room, where they were examined and left for further research and identification.

A mini-archive has now been set up, to which POSA members have donated photographs, documents and other interesting items of memorabilia. Betty Moisley provided notes about the beginning of both the College and POSA. Bill Buckley provided comments on his time as Director. As a student in the early 1950s, I had my own memories and photographs and other memorabilia. I also had in my possession the first and second books of the Minutes of Committee Meetings and Annual General Meetings of the Association, as well as the current Minutes book. So I began reading through and picking out relevant dates and pieces of information, until a skeleton account of the life and times of Padgate was written. After some discussion, the Committee decided to delay the printing of the booklet for twelve months, in order to give other interested POSA members time to contribute their personal memories.

The aim was to give an interesting picture of life at the College during the six decades of its existence, and a broader outline of the developments carried out at Padgate from its beginning to the present day. I am grateful to those who accepted the challenge, particularly Hilary Tucker, who provided much information about events during her years at Padgate. She also read the first and second drafts of the text, correcting some misinformation and explaining the most recent developments. Without her valuable help, this work would not present such a complete picture. I am mindful that information on some periods is sketchy, to say the least, and in some cases non-existent. I can only apologise and admit that I was unable to obtain relevant details. Readers of this work who wish to do so can still contribute items or information to the Padgate Archive. Submissions will be gratefully accepted and carefully stored.

It has recently been suggested to me, by an elderly local resident, that there were no Canadians at Padgate; they were Americans. If that is so, how did the name 'Canada Hall' arise? That remains a puzzle, although research via the Warrington-Worldwide news website discovered that the name may have been applied only to the theatre. In that case, the question remains, why? Maybe we will never know. It is my hope that this book will revive happy memories for former students and staff, and give to everyone who reads it a view of an establishment where only the best was encouraged and achieved.

E.R.N. - January 2007.

CONTRIBUTORS...

Grateful thanks are due to the following contributors who responded to the appeal for memories, or who supplied memorabilia from which information was obtained:

Cyril (Sid/Bill) Bailey
Ben Barrett
Bill Buckley
Eileen Coulson
Norma Cousins
Pat Eagle
Tanya Eastwood
Mavis Fielding
Helen Henwood
Janet Hobbs
Betty Moisley
Jonathan Moores
Dr Malcolm Rhodes
Vera Singleton
Andy Slater
Dr Alan Smith
Hilary Tucker
Karen Willis.

The text was prepared for publication by Iain Ramsay, a second year Marketing Student, as part of his Work Based Learning module at the University of Chester.